Internet Field Tri

W9-AOA-547

An Online Visit to
AFRICA

File Edit View Go Bookmarks Communicator Help

Back Forward Reload Home Search Images Print Security Stop

Netsite: What's Related

Erin M. Hovanec

The Rosen Publishing Group's
PowerKids Press™
New York

For O

Published in 2001 by The Rosen Publishing Group, Inc.

29 East 21st Street, New York, NY 10010

First Edition

Book Design: Maria Melendez

Photo Credits: Cover, title page, p. 7, 8, 16 © H. Armstrong Roberts; Title page © Chase Swift/CORBIS; Title page, 15 © Digital Stock; Title page © RubberBall Productions; p. 11 © Chinch Gryniewicz; Ecoscene/CORBIS; p. 12 © Galen Rowell/CORBIS; p. 19 © Superstock; p. 20 © Charles & Josette Lenars/CORBIS.

Hovanec, Erin M.
    An online visit to Africa / Erin M. Hovanec.
        p. cm.— (Internet field trips)
    Includes index.
    Summary: An online trip to various Internet web sites reveals a variety of facts about the continent of Africa.
    ISBN 0-8239-5651-2 (alk. paper)
    1. Africa—Juvenile literature. [1. Africa.] I. Title.
DT22 .H68 2000
960—dc21   00-021996

Manufactured in the United States of America

Contents

File   Edit   View   Go   Bookmarks   Communicator   Help   2:37 PM

Back   Forward   Reload   Home   Search   Images   Print   Security   Stop

Netsite: What's Related

Let's Get Started

You might have all the tools that you will need to search the Internet from your home. If you don't, you can go to your school library or public library to get on the Web. Here's what you'll need:

A personal computer
Personal computers have a monitor (also called a screen), a mouse, and a keyboard.

A modem
A modem connects your computer to the telephone line and then to other computers. Some computers have built-in modems.

A telephone connection
Your modem talks to other computers through a telephone line.

Internet software
These are programs that tell your computer how to use the Internet.

An Internet Service Provider
These companies allow you to get on the Internet. They usually charge a fee every month or year.

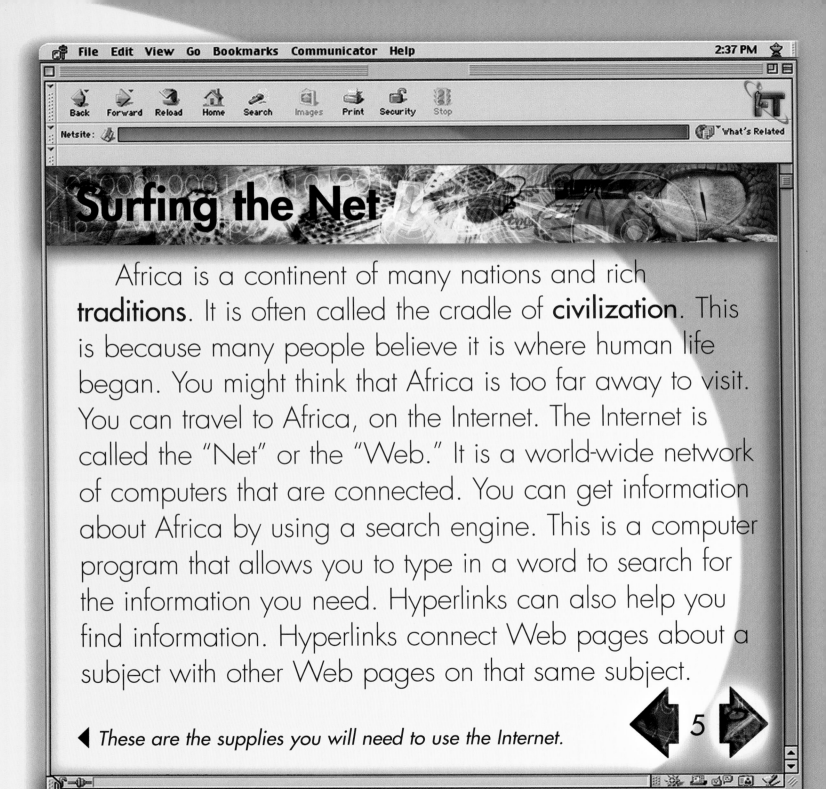

Surfing the Net

Africa is a continent of many nations and rich **traditions**. It is often called the cradle of **civilization**. This is because many people believe it is where human life began. You might think that Africa is too far away to visit. You can travel to Africa, on the Internet. The Internet is called the "Net" or the "Web." It is a world-wide network of computers that are connected. You can get information about Africa by using a search engine. This is a computer program that allows you to type in a word to search for the information you need. Hyperlinks can also help you find information. Hyperlinks connect Web pages about a subject with other Web pages on that same subject.

These are the supplies you will need to use the Internet.

Searching for "Africa"

Africa is the second largest of the seven continents on Earth. Only the continent of Asia is bigger. Africa is nearly 12 million square miles (31 million sq km) in size. That's about four times the size of the United States! On a map, you can see that Africa is south of Europe and Asia. The Atlantic Ocean is to the west. The Indian Ocean is to the east. About one in every eight people on Earth lives in Africa. This means that about 750 million people live in Africa.

If you want to find out more fun facts about Africa, check out Africa Geographia at http://www.geographia.com/indx06.htm.

6

Here is a globe showing the outline of Africa and a picture of the Nile River, the longest river on Earth.

To learn more facts about Africa:
http://www.library.thinkquest.org/16645/the_land/the_land.shtml
http://www.ihik12.oh.us.htm

File   Edit   View   Go   Bookmarks   Communicator   Help   2:37 PM

Back   Forward   Reload   Home   Search   Images   Print   Security   Stop

Netsite: What's Related

To learn more facts about Africa's weather:
http://www.weather.com
htp://www.weather.com/intl/regions_index/Africa_region.html

What's the Weather?

What's the weather like in Africa? Web sites can give the weather and forecasts for Africa's countries and cities. Most of Africa has a very warm or hot climate. Ninety percent of Africa is in the **tropics**. This is because the **equator** runs right through Africa. Many places are very hot during the day then become cool at night. It even snows in the mountains. Most of Africa has seasons of heavy rain. Liberia and other countries on Africa's west coast receive more than 100 inches (254 cm) of rainfall a year. That's a lot of rain! In parts of the Sahara Desert, rain may fall only every six or seven years! Some young children living in the desert have never even seen rain.

◀ *Africa's highest temperatures occur in the Sahara Desert.*

Mapping It Out

Africa is so big that it contains many different kinds of people and places. You can visit these people and places. Just click your mouse! You can travel to towering mountains and wide grasslands, tropical rain forests, and dry deserts.

The continent of Africa is divided into 53 different countries. Several nearby islands are also considered a part of Africa. The Sudan is the largest country in Africa. It is more than 5,000 times larger than the Seychelles, Africa's smallest country. The Seychelles is really a group of 85 islands. Nigeria is the country with the largest population. Nigeria has 120 million people.

Africa's rain forests are home to many plants and animals. ▶

To learn more about Africa's geography:
http://www.nationalgeographic.com/xpeditions/main.html
http://www.lib.utexas.edu/Libs/PCL/Map_collection/africa.html

To learn more about the Sahara Desert:http://www.ontheline.org.uk/ explore/nature/deserts/sahara.htm. Learn about Kilimanjaro: http://www.gorp.com/gorp/location/africa.tanzania/home_kil.htm

Back   Forward   Reload   Home   Search   Images   Print   Security   Stop

Netsite: What's Related

Nature's Wonders

You can find some of nature's biggest and most beautiful creations in Africa. Did you know that Africa's desert, the Sahara, is the world's largest desert? It covers one-fourth of Africa and is almost as big as the United States! About two-fifths of Africa is made up of grasslands called **savannas**. Savannas are home to many of Africa's most interesting animals.

The world's longest river, the Nile, is also in Africa. It flows more than 4,160 miles (6,486 km). Mount Kilimanjaro in Tanzania is the highest peak in Africa. At 19,340 feet (5,895 m), it is one of the world's tallest mountains. This mountain is actually an inactive volcano.

◀ *Snow covers glaciers on Mount Kilimanjaro year-round.*

13

Amazing Animals!

Many people go on **safari** in Africa to take photos of animals in their natural surroundings. Go on safari to Animal Planet's Web site at http://animal.discovery.com. Africa's savannas are home to many different kinds of animals. Savanna animals include cheetahs, elephants, giraffes, lions, rhinoceroses, and zebras. Crocodiles, flamingoes, hippopotamuses, lizards, and snakes live in tropical lakes, rivers, and swamps. African rain forests are filled with chimpanzees, gorillas, monkeys, and wild pigs.

Some African animals are in danger of becoming **extinct**. Many African countries have created **game preserves** and national parks to keep animals safe.

Many African countries have laws against hunting. These laws protect animals like this cheetah. ▶

To learn more about Africa's animals:
http://www.nationalgeographic.com/wildlife/
http://www.africa.com/interacton/afri_info/birding

To learn more about the people in Africa:
http://www.odci.gov/cia/publications/factbook
http://pbs.org/wonders/globalnav.htm

One Continent,
MANY PEOPLES

Africa has many countries and many different kinds of people. More than 3,000 different **ethnic groups** live on this continent. More than 800 languages are spoken in Africa. One language, Swahili, is spoken mostly in Kenya, Tanzania, and Zaire. These countries are in East Africa. Sudan is in North Africa. Most of the people who live in the country of Sudan speak Arabic.

Millions of Africans live in cities, but many more live in the countryside. In **rural** Africa, many people still follow the **customs** of their **ancestors**. Religion is an important part of life in Africa. Most Africans practice Islam, Christianity, or traditional African religions.

This is a picture of African children wearing traditional clothing.

17

African Industries

Agriculture, which includes farming and raising livestock, is the biggest **industry** in Africa. Many Africans support themselves and their families by raising camels, goats, cattle, and sheep. Africa produces more cocoa beans, cashews, vanilla beans, and yams than anywhere else in the world. This continent also provides much of the world's bananas, coffee, cotton, peanuts, rubber, sugar, and teas.

Africa also has rich **minerals** that are sold around the world. Africa ships its natural **resources**, which include gold, copper, iron ore, diamonds, oil, and natural gas, all over the world.

This is a gold mine in South Africa. ▶

File   Edit   View   Go   Bookmarks   Communicator   Help   2:37 PM

Back   Forward   Reload   Home   Search   Images   Print   Security   Stop

Netsite: What's Related

For more interesting facts about Africa, go to the African Information Center at: http://www.hmnet.com/africa/1africa.html
http://www.Africa.com

To learn more about African art:
http://www.lib.virginia.edu/dic/93.ray.aa/Exhibition.html
http://www.ethnographica.com

Art and Music

For thousands of years, Africans have created dazzling works of art. The Web site of the Smithsonian Institution's National Museum of African Art at http:www.si.edu/nmafa/ has information on African art throughout history. African artists are praised for their work making baskets, beads, cloth, glass, leather, metal work, and pottery. African sculptors create masks and figures. African music has a wide range of styles. Musicians sing and **chant** and play instruments such as drums, flutes, horns, and pipes. African storytellers share histories and stories to teach listeners important lessons about African customs.

◀ *African dancers and musicians often wear traditional masks and costumes.*

 21

Surf Some More!

   Africa is a huge continent filled with natural wonders, unusual animals, and fascinating people. It is also a place that is always changing. You can surf the Internet to find out about those changes as soon as they happen. To discover more about Africa today, check out AfricaNews Online at http://www.africanews.org. You can also try, http://www.afroam.org/children/children.html. From lakes like Lakes Victoria or Tanganyika, to countries like Liberia, it's all on the Web! You'll never run out of things to see and learn.

GLOSSARY

ancestors (AN-ses-turz) Relatives who lived long ago.

chant (CHANT) To say words over and over again, as in a religious service.

civilization (sih-vih-lih-ZAY-shun) A group of people living within one country.

customs (KUS-tumz) The accepted, respected ways of doing something that are passed down from parent to child.

equator (ih-KWAY-tur) An imaginary line around Earth that separates it into two parts, north and south. The area around the equator is always hot.

ethnic groups (ETH-nik GROOPS) Groups of people, each having the same race, culture, or language, or belonging to the same country.

extinct (ik-STINKT) To no longer exist.

game preserves (GAYM prih-ZERVZ) Areas of land that are set aside for wild animals to live in.

industry (IN-des-tree) A business that makes a product or provides a service.

mineral (MIH-ner-ul) A natural ingredient from Earth's soil, such as coal or copper, that comes from the ground and is not a plant, animal, or other living thing.

resources (REE-sors-ez) A supply or source of energy or useful materials.

rural (RUR-ul) In the country or in a farming area.

safari (suh-FAHR-ee) A journey through Africa to see the land and animals.

savannas (suh-VA-nuhs) Areas of grassland with few trees or bushes.

traditions (truh-DIH-shunz) Ways of doing something that are passed down through the years.

tropics (TRAH-piks) The warm parts of Earth near the equator.

23

Index

Web Sites

There are lots of exciting Web Sites about Africa. Check them out on the following pages: pp, 6, 7, 8, 11, 12, 14, 15, 16, 19, 20, 21, and 22.